DATE:

Stick your

favourite picture here...

PREDICTIONS	RESEMBLANCE
D.O.B - In June	MOSTLY MOM [x]
WEIGHT - A lot	
TIME - during the day	DEFINITELY DAD [ ]
EYES - 2 of them	
HAIR - I hope so	

MESSAGE FOR BABY

You're in for a crazy ride kid.

my best advice

Don't second guess your instincts... he'll be just fine.

lots of love from....
Shaysha

PREDICTIONS	RESEMBLANCE
D.O.B - JUN 25	MOSTLY MOM ☑
WEIGHT - 8.5	
TIME - 4:30 AM	DEFINITELY DAD ☐
EYES - blue	
HAIR - red	

MESSAGE FOR BABY

I am going to love you the best -- besides your Mom + Dad

my best advice

Patience.

lots of love from....
MeMe

PREDICTIONS

D.O.B - June 23rd
WEIGHT - 7 lbs 3 ounces
TIME - 8:30 am
EYES - blue
HAIR - brown

RESEMBLANCE

MOSTLY MOM ☑
DEFINITELY DAD ☐

MESSAGE FOR BABY

my best advice

Pamper yourself when you can. You will be a great mom. I'm very excited for you and your husband. Can't wait to meet him ♡

lots of love from....

Julie Turkington

PREDICTIONS	RESEMBLANCE
D.O.B - June 10th	MOSTLY MOM [½]
WEIGHT - 10 lbs	
TIME - 4:25 pm	DEFINITELY DAD [½]
EYES - Blue	
HAIR - Brown	

MESSAGE FOR BABY

You are a gift from a higher power! You are so loved!

my best advice

Talk to one another!

lots of love from....
Katlyn + Sean

PREDICTIONS		RESEMBLANCE	
D.O.B - 6/17/20			
WEIGHT - 7.5 lbs		MOSTLY MOM	½
TIME - 4:32 pm		DEFINITELY DAD	½
EYES - Hazel			
HAIR - Brown			

MESSAGE FOR BABY

Know you are always loved and blessed!

my best advice

Blow lots of raspberries on each other!

lots of love from....

Caitlin + Joel

PREDICTIONS

D.O.B - 6/19/20
WEIGHT - 9 lb. 0 oz
TIME - 12:30 pm
EYES - brown
HAIR - blonde

RESEMBLANCE

MOSTLY MOM ☐
DEFINITELY DAD ✓

MESSAGE FOR BABY

Can't wait to meet my grandson! ♡

my best advice

Don't sweat the small stuff, because it will ALL be small stuff!

lots of love from....
Gramma Kelly
& Grampa Steve

PREDICTIONS

- **D.O.B-** 6/22
- **WEIGHT-** 8lbs
- **TIME-** 2pm
- **EYES-** green
- **HAIR-** Red

RESEMBLANCE

- MOSTLY MOM [ ]
- DEFINITELY DAD [X]

MESSAGE FOR BABY

We are all so excited to meet you ♡

my best advice

Don't worry, be happy :) ♡

lots of love from....

Skylar ♡

PREDICTIONS

D.O.B - 6/15/20
WEIGHT - 8 lbs
TIME - 4 am
EYES - brown
HAIR - brown

RESEMBLANCE

MOSTLY MOM ☐
DEFINITELY DAD ☑

MESSAGE FOR BABY

So excited to meet you!

my best advice

Congratulations Ashlynn + Keith! Good luck with everything and I hope you have an easy delivery!

lots of love from....
♡ Vanessa

PREDICTIONS	RESEMBLANCE
D.O.B- 6/30/20	MOSTLY MOM ✓
WEIGHT- 10 LBS	
TIME- 6:30 am	DEFINITELY DAD ☐
EYES- Green/Gray	
HAIR- Dark Brown	

MESSAGE FOR BABY

Can't wait for you to join us in this world ♡

my best advice

Congradulations
I know that y'all are going to be rockin parents so happy for you

lots of love from....
Julissa ♡

PREDICTIONS

D.O.B - July 1
WEIGHT - 8.5
TIME - 10pm
EYES - Blue
HAIR - Red/Blonde

RESEMBLANCE

m

MOSTLY MOM ☑

DEFINITELY DAD ☐

MESSAGE FOR BABY

Welcome Player #3!

my best advice

Always be on the same page. (Mom says NO, Dad says NO.)

lots of love from....

Stephanie ♡

PREDICTIONS

D.O.B-

WEIGHT-

TIME-

EYES-

HAIR-

RESEMBLANCE

MOSTLY MOM ☐

DEFINITELY DAD ☐

MESSAGE FOR BABY

my best advice

lots of love from....

PREDICTIONS	RESEMBLANCE
D.O.B -	
WEIGHT -	MOSTLY MOM ☐
TIME -	
EYES -	DEFINITELY DAD ☐
HAIR -	

MESSAGE FOR BAby

my best advice

lots of love from....

PREDICTIONS	RESEMBLANCE
D.O.B-	
WEIGHT-	MOSTLY MOM ☐
TIME-	DEFINITELY DAD ☐
EYES-	
HAIR-	

MESSAGE FOR BABY

my best advice

lots of love from....

PREDICTIONS	RESEMBLANCE
D.O.B-	
WEIGHT-	MOSTLY MOM ☐
TIME-	DEFINITELY DAD ☐
EYES-	
HAIR-	

MESSAGE FOR BABY

my best advice

lots of love from....

PREDICTIONS	RESEMBLANCE
D.O.B -	
WEIGHT -	MOSTLY MOM ☐
TIME -	
EYES -	DEFINITELY DAD ☐
HAIR -	

MESSAGE FOR BABY

my best advice

lots of love from....

PREDICTIONS   RESEMBLANCE

D.O.B -

WEIGHT -   MOSTLY MOM ☐

TIME -

                    DEFINITELY DAD ☐
EYES -

HAIR -

MESSAGE FOR BABY

my best advice

lots of love from....

PREDICTIONS	RESEMBLANCE
D.O.B -	
WEIGHT -	MOSTLY MOM ☐
TIME -	DEFINITELY DAD ☐
EYES -	
HAIR -	

MESSAGE FOR BABY

my best advice

lots of love from....

PREDICTIONS	RESEMBLANCE
D.O.B -	
WEIGHT -	MOSTLY MOM ☐
TIME -	
EYES -	DEFINITELY DAD ☐
HAIR -	

MESSAGE FOR BABY

my best advice

lots of love from....

PREDICTIONS   RESEMBLANCE

D.O.B -
                     MOSTLY
WEIGHT -   MOM   ☐

TIME -
                     DEFINITELY
EYES -   DAD   ☐

HAIR -

MESSAGE FOR BABY

my best advice

lots of love from....

PREDICTIONS   RESEMBLANCE

D.O.B -

WEIGHT -   MOSTLY MOM ☐

TIME -
                  DEFINITELY DAD ☐
EYES -

HAIR -

MESSAGE FOR BABY

my best advice

lots of love from....

PREDICTIONS

RESEMBLANCE

D.O.B -

WEIGHT -

MOSTLY MOM ☐

TIME -

DEFINITELY DAD ☐

EYES -

HAIR -

MESSAGE FOR BABY

my best advice

lots of love from....

PREDICTIONS   RESEMBLANCE

D.O.B -
                     MOSTLY
WEIGHT -   MOM   ☐

TIME -
                     DEFINITELY
EYES -   DAD   ☐

HAIR -

MESSAGE FOR BABY

---

my best advice

lots of love from....

PREDICTIONS

RESEMBLANCE

D.O.B -

WEIGHT -

MOSTLY MOM ☐

TIME -

DEFINITELY DAD ☐

EYES -

HAIR -

MESSAGE FOR BABY

my best advice

lots of love from....

PREDICTIONS	RESEMBLANCE
D.O.B-	
WEIGHT-	MOSTLY MOM ☐
TIME-	
EYES-	DEFINITELY DAD ☐
HAIR-	

MESSAGE FOR BABY

my best advice

lots of love from....

PREDICTIONS

RESEMBLANCE

D.O.B -

WEIGHT -

TIME -

EYES -

HAIR -

MOSTLY MOM ☐

DEFINITELY DAD ☐

MESSAGE FOR BABY

my best advice

lots of love from....

PREDICTIONS   RESEMBLANCE

D.O.B -

WEIGHT -   MOSTLY MOM ☐

TIME -   DEFINITELY DAD ☐

EYES -

HAIR -

MESSAGE FOR BABY

my best advice

lots of love from....

PREDICTIONS   RESEMBLANCE

D.O.B -

WEIGHT -   MOSTLY MOM ☐

TIME -   DEFINITELY DAD ☐

EYES -

HAIR -

MESSAGE FOR BABY

my best advice

lots of love from....

PREDICTIONS	RESEMBLANCE
D.O.B-	
WEIGHT-	MOSTLY MOM ☐
TIME-	DEFINITELY DAD ☐
EYES-	
HAIR-	

MESSAGE FOR BABY

my best advice

lots of love from....

PREDICTIONS	RESEMBLANCE
D.O.B-	
WEIGHT-	MOSTLY MOM ☐
TIME-	
EYES-	DEFINITELY DAD ☐
HAIR-	

MESSAGE FOR BABY

my best advice

lots of love from....

PREDICTIONS	RESEMBLANCE
D.O.B -	
WEIGHT -	☐ MOSTLY MOM
TIME -	☐ DEFINITELY DAD
EYES -	
HAIR -	

MESSAGE FOR BAFY

my best advice

lots of love from....

PREDICTIONS	RESEMBLANCE
D.O.B -	MOSTLY MOM ☐
WEIGHT -	
TIME -	DEFINITELY DAD ☐
EYES -	
HAIR -	

MESSAGE FOR BABY

my best advice

lots of love from....

PREDICTIONS   RESEMBLANCE

D.O.B-

WEIGHT-   MOSTLY MOM ☐

TIME-

EYES-   DEFINITELY DAD ☐

HAIR-

MESSAGE FOR BABY

my best advice

lots of love from....

PREDICTIONS

RESEMBLANCE

D.O.B -

WEIGHT -

TIME -

EYES -

HAIR -

MOSTLY MOM ☐

DEFINITELY DAD ☐

MESSAGE FOR BABY

my best advice

lots of love from....

PREDICTIONS	RESEMBLANCE
D.O.B-	MOSTLY MOM ☐
WEIGHT-	
TIME-	DEFINITELY DAD ☐
EYES-	
HAIR-	

MESSAGE FOR BABY

my best advice

lots of love from....

PREDICTIONS   RESEMBLANCE

D.O.B -

                     MOSTLY
WEIGHT -   MOM   ☐

TIME -
                     DEFINITELY
                     DAD   ☐
EYES -

HAIR -

MESSAGE FOR BABY

my best advice

lots of love from....

PREDICTIONS   RESEMBLANCE

D.O.B -

WEIGHT -   ☐ MOSTLY MOM

TIME -

EYES -   ☐ DEFINITELY DAD

HAIR -

MESSAGE FOR BABY

my best advice

lots of love from....

PREDICTIONS   RESEMBLANCE

D.O.B -
                     MOSTLY MOM ☐
WEIGHT -

TIME -
                     DEFINITELY DAD ☐
EYES -

HAIR -

MESSAGE FOR BABY

my best advice

lots of love from....

PREDICTIONS RESEMBLANCE

D.O.B -

WEIGHT -   MOSTLY MOM ☐

TIME -

                   DEFINITELY DAD ☐
EYES -

HAIR -

MESSAGE FOR BAZY

my best advice

lots of love from....

PREDICTIONS	RESEMBLANCE
D.O.B-	
WEIGHT-	MOSTLY MOM ☐
TIME-	
EYES-	DEFINITELY DAD ☐
HAIR-	

MESSAGE FOR BABY

my best advice

lots of love from....

PREDICTIONS

RESEMBLANCE

D.O.B -

WEIGHT -

MOSTLY MOM ☐

TIME -

DEFINITELY DAD ☐

EYES -

HAIR -

MESSAGE FOR BABY

my best advice

lots of love from....

PREDICTIONS

RESEMBLANCE

D.O.B -

WEIGHT -

☐ MOSTLY MOM

TIME -

☐ DEFINITELY DAD

EYES -

HAIR -

MESSAGE FOR BABY

my best advice

lots of love from....

PREDICTIONS   RESEMBLANCE

D.O.B -
                MOSTLY MOM ☐
WEIGHT -

TIME -
                DEFINITELY DAD ☐
EYES -

HAIR -

MESSAGE FOR BABY

my best advice

lots of love from....

PREDICTIONS	RESEMBLANCE
D.O.B -	
WEIGHT -	MOSTLY MOM ☐
TIME -	DEFINITELY DAD ☐
EYES -	
HAIR -	

MESSAGE FOR BABY

my best advice

lots of love from....

PREDICTIONS	RESEMBLANCE
D.O.B-	
WEIGHT-	MOSTLY MOM ☐
TIME-	DEFINITELY DAD ☐
EYES-	
HAIR-	

MESSAGE FOR BABY

my best advice

lots of love from....

PREDICTIONS   RESEMBLANCE

D.O.B-

WEIGHT-   MOSTLY MOM ☐

TIME-
                    DEFINITELY DAD ☐
EYES-

HAIR-

MESSAGE FOR BABY

my best advice

lots of love from....

PREDICTIONS   RESEMBLANCE

D.O.B -

WEIGHT -   MOSTLY
                             MOM ☐

TIME -
                          DEFINITELY
                             DAD ☐
EYES -

HAIR -

MESSAGE FOR BAZY

my best advice

lots of love from....

PREDICTIONS   RESEMBLANCE

D.O.B-

WEIGHT-   MOSTLY MOM ☐

TIME-
                DEFINITELY DAD ☐
EYES-

HAIR-

MESSAGE FOR BABY

my best advice

lots of love from....

PREDICTIONS   RESEMBLANCE

D.O.B -
                     MOSTLY MOM ☐
WEIGHT -

TIME -
                     DEFINITELY DAD ☐
EYES -

HAIR -

MESSAGE FOR BAZBY

my best advice

lots of love from....

PREDICTIONS	RESEMBLANCE
D.O.B -	
WEIGHT -	MOSTLY MOM ☐
TIME -	DEFINITELY DAD ☐
EYES -	
HAIR -	

MESSAGE FOR BABY

my best advice

lots of love from....

PREDICTIONS   RESEMBLANCE

D.O.B-
                     MOSTLY MOM ☐
WEIGHT-

TIME-   DEFINITELY DAD ☐

EYES-

HAIR-

MESSAGE FOR BABY

my best advice

lots of love from....

PREDICTIONS   RESEMBLANCE

D.O.B -
                  MOSTLY
WEIGHT -   MOM   ☐

TIME -
                  DEFINITELY
EYES -   DAD   ☐

HAIR -

MESSAGE FOR BABY

my best advice

lots of love from....

PREDICTIONS   RESEMBLANCE

D.O.B -
              MOSTLY
WEIGHT -   MOM   ☐

TIME -
              DEFINITELY
EYES -   DAD   ☐

HAIR -

MESSAGE FOR BABY

my best advice

lots of love from....

PREDICTIONS

RESEMBLANCE

D.O.B -

WEIGHT -

MOSTLY MOM ☐

TIME -

DEFINITELY DAD ☐

EYES -

HAIR -

MESSAGE FOR BABY

my best advice

lots of love from....

PREDICTIONS	RESEMBLANCE
D.O.B-	
WEIGHT-	☐ MOSTLY MOM
TIME-	
EYES-	☐ DEFINITELY DAD
HAIR-	

MESSAGE FOR BABY

my best advice from....

PREDICTIONS	RESEMBLANCE
D.O.B -	
WEIGHT -	MOSTLY MOM ☐
TIME -	
EYES -	DEFINITELY DAD ☐
HAIR -	

MESSAGE FOR BABY

my best advice

lots of love from....

PREDICTIONS   RESEMBLANCE

D.O.B -

WEIGHT -   MOSTLY MOM ☐

TIME -   DEFINITELY DAD ☐

EYES -

HAIR -

MESSAGE FOR BABY

my best advice

lots of love from....

PREDICTIONS	RESEMBLANCE
D.O.B-	
WEIGHT-	MOSTLY MOM ☐
TIME-	DEFINITELY DAD ☐
EYES-	
HAIR-	

MESSAGE FOR BABY

my best advice

lots of love from....

PREDICTIONS   RESEMBLANCE

D.O.B -
                     MOSTLY
WEIGHT -   MOM   ☐

TIME -
                     DEFINITELY
EYES -   DAD   ☐

HAIR -

MESSAGE FOR BABY

my best advice

lots of love from....

PREDICTIONS	RESEMBLANCE
D.O.B -	
WEIGHT -	MOSTLY MOM ☐
TIME -	
EYES -	DEFINITELY DAD ☐
HAIR -	

MESSAGE FOR BABY

my best advice

lots of love from....

PREDICTIONS RESEMBLANCE

D.O.B-
WEIGHT-   MOSTLY MOM ☐
TIME-
           DEFINITELY DAD ☐
EYES-
HAIR-

MESSAGE FOR BAZY

my best advice

lots of love from....

PREDICTIONS	RESEMBLANCE
D.O.B -	
WEIGHT -	MOSTLY MOM ☐
TIME -	DEFINITELY DAD ☐
EYES -	
HAIR -	

MESSAGE FOR BABY

my best advice

lots of love from....

PREDICTIONS	RESEMBLANCE
D.O.B -	MOSTLY MOM ☐
WEIGHT -	
TIME -	DEFINITELY DAD ☐
EYES -	
HAIR -	

MESSAGE FOR BABY

my best advice

lots of love from....

PREDICTIONS

D.O.B -

WEIGHT -

TIME -

EYES -

HAIR -

RESEMBLANCE

☐ MOSTLY MOM

☐ DEFINITELY DAD

MESSAGE FOR BABY

my best advice

lots of love from....

PREDICTIONS	RESEMBLANCE
D.O.B -	
WEIGHT -	☐ MOSTLY MOM
TIME -	
EYES -	☐ DEFINITELY DAD
HAIR -	

MESSAGE FOR BABY

my best advice

lots of love from....

PREDICTIONS	RESEMBLANCE
D.O.B -	
WEIGHT -	MOSTLY MOM ☐
TIME -	
EYES -	DEFINITELY DAD ☐
HAIR -	

MESSAGE FOR BABY

my best advice

lots of love from....

PREDICTIONS	RESEMBLANCE
D.O.B -	
WEIGHT -	MOSTLY MOM ☐
TIME -	
EYES -	DEFINITELY DAD ☐
HAIR -	

MESSAGE FOR BABY

my best advice

lots of love from....

PREDICTIONS	RESEMBLANCE
D.O.B -	
WEIGHT -	MOSTLY MOM ☐
TIME -	DEFINITELY DAD ☐
EYES -	
HAIR -	

MESSAGE FOR BAGY

my best advice

lots of love from....

PREDICTIONS	RESEMBLANCE
D.O.B-	
WEIGHT-	MOSTLY MOM ☐
TIME-	DEFINITELY DAD ☐
EYES-	
HAIR-	

MESSAGE FOR BABY

my best advice

lots of love from....

GIFT LOG

FROM:	GIFT DESCRIPTION	THANK YOU SENT

Gift Log

From:	Gift Description	Thank You Sent

Gift Log

From:	Gift Description	Thank You Sent

Gift Log

From:	Gift Description	Thank You Sent

Gift Log

From:	Gift Description	Thank You Sent